DAPI DAUGHTERS

YOUR
INFLUENCE
YOUR PURE INNOCENCE

MY
DECISION
MOMMY WILL PROTECT

YOUR INFLUENCE
INSPIRES ME TO BREAK THIS CYCLE.

YOUR INFLUENCE INSPIRES ME TO BREAK THIS CYCLE.

YOUR INFLUENCE, MY DECISION

Published by: I AM RONIESHA SEATON, LLC.

All *rights reserved.*

No parts of this book may be reproduced in any form or by any electronic or mechanical means, including information storage and retrieval systems, without written permission from the author, except for the use of brief quotations in a book review.

Authors and credits: Nathalie Alvarado, Ta'Shay Todd, Jordyn Sephes, Carmela Martin, Ava kerwin, Yamia Brown, Daniela Morales, Deja Perry, Tifani Sanchez-Romero, Hayden McCall-Ross, Roniesha Seaton, and Delaware Adolescent Program, Inc. staff

Cover Design: I Am Roniesha Seaton, LLC

Photography (student portraits): Jonhny Rocket

For bulk purchases contact Roniesha Seaton at
Info@iamronieshaseaton.com

ISBN: 979-8-9906673-3-4

© 2025 Roniesha Seaton

YOUR INFLUENCE
INSPIRES ME TO BREAK THIS CYCLE.

CONTENTS

Acknowledgment………………………..5

Introduction ……………………….....7

Foreword………………………………10

Shifting Paths…………………………13

My Truth, His Future…………………..19

For The Son I Carried, For the Father I Lost …………………………...…………….23

The Beginning of My Journey as A Girl Mom…………………………………….29

Unplanned Blessings and Valuable Lessons……………….………………..35

Breaking The Cycle: A Promise to My Child………………………………. ….43

Where Does Big Emotions Go……………………………………...47

My Promise to Her: Evolving to Be the Best Mom I Can Be …………...…………53

Baby Steps on Brand New Trails...….......63

YOUR INFLUENCE
INSPIRES ME TO BREAK THIS CYCLE.

This I Believe ………………………...69

Breaking Cycles………………....….77

YOUR INFLUENCE
INSPIRES ME TO BREAK THIS CYCLE.

ACKNOWLEDGEMENT

With profound appreciation, I announce and thank everyone involved in the making of this project! First, thank you to Delaware Adolescent Program, Inc. (DAPI), for welcoming me into your district and trusting my leadership. Thank you, Dr. Doris Griffin, Executive Director of DAPI, for trusting me to teach social and emotional learning practices to an excellent group of young ladies. I am grateful for your guidance, understanding, and invaluable leadership. Thank you for helping to mold my vision and for being cooperative and championing a project that will have a dynamic and lasting impact on these young ladies for the rest of their lives.

Deputy Director at DAPI, teachers, and staff. Thanks for the unrestricted and unwavering support you have given as a collective. You all welcomed me into DAPI with open arms and genuine kindness. I have been blessed to have shared my time and space with remarkable people who assisted

YOUR INFLUENCE
INSPIRES ME TO BREAK THIS CYCLE.

me in ensuring that our girls received superior care and inspiration.

To my daughter Honesty Seaton, thank you. Your influence on me as a teen mom helped me excel in my mission to change the narrative around teen pregnancy. Thank you, Danta Taylor, for the abundant support you've provided behind the scenes.

Jonhny Rocket and all my family and friends. Thank you! You have all supported me from the beginning and have been a powerful support team.

Lastly, I would personally like to thank each parent! If it had not been for the amazing gift, you've given this world, in your daughters, this would not have been possible. Thank you for allowing me to provide guidance and counsel to your children. It truly takes a village. Thank you for allowing me to be a part of your village!

Alone we can do little; together, we can do so much more! The greatest impact happens when we all work together with one mission in mind, service!

YOUR INFLUENCE
INSPIRES ME TO BREAK THIS CYCLE.

INTRODUCTION

Your Influence, My Decision: *A Conscious Choice to Break Family Cycles for Future Generations*

Recognizing when you are repeating a cycle can often be one of the most difficult realizations to make. For generations, these cycles have been unconsciously repeated, leaving the next child to endure the suffering of unresolved trauma that can lead to harmful parenting behaviors.

This year, I had the opportunity to teach a course on violence prevention in relation to maternal health. One of the segments focused on "Exposed Child Syndrome," also known as Trauma-exposed Children. This condition can lead to a variety of mental and physical health challenges, such as PTSD, depression, anxiety, and behavioral issues stemming from repeated exposure to traumatic events.

Teen pregnancy frequently reflects a cycle of some kind. Each new and expectant

YOUR INFLUENCE INSPIRES ME TO BREAK THIS CYCLE.

mother was encouraged to write a story about a cycle they wish to break for their child—one that was less than ideal for them during their own childhood. This exercise challenged them to revisit their less favorable experiences, allowing them to put in words their feelings and actively work toward ensuring that their children do not endure similar suffering.

As you turn each page, you might be surprised by some of the traumatic experiences shared. The goal of each story is to raise awareness about various hardships. We hope that these narratives inspire you to break any negative cycles you may be caught in.

Every word has strength, every sentence has vulnerability, every paragraph has healing, and every story has a message! These ladies can't and won't be stopped! The unlimited potential and creativity within each young lady will carry them to heights beyond their wildest imagination. This is just the beginning.

YOUR INFLUENCE INSPIRES ME TO BREAK THIS CYCLE.

Disclaimer: Parents, please read each story with an unbiased, nonjudgmental mind. Be open to receiving each story and remember that you once were where they are. Look at each story as a conversation starter with your child. Please try not to take anything personally, as some, but not all, stories contain raw emotions. Some may find the stories triggering. If you read something you weren't aware of, now is the time to show support and love for your child.

Remember, our children belong to us, but they are not us! They won't always think the ways we do; they won't always make us proud, and they will make mistakes. If we continue to love our children, they will eventually come around, bringing all of life's lessons full circle. Don't give up on your baby! She's finding her true self.

- Love Ms. Seaton

YOUR INFLUENCE
INSPIRES ME TO BREAK THIS CYCLE.

FOREWORD

I am deeply honored and filled with anticipation to pen the foreword for this collection of short stories, a testament to the strength and resilience of our DAPI Daughters. These young women, our DAPI Daughters, are not just capable, they are extraordinary.

I am so grateful to the authors of these stories for sharing their experiences. Their stories are honest, heartwarming, and sometimes heartbreaking, but they are all stories of hope and resilience. This book will help raise awareness of teen parenting challenges and inspire other young parents to know they are not alone.

Many resources are available to help teen parents succeed. Some programs can help with financial assistance, childcare, and education. There are also support groups where teen parents can connect with other parents with similar experiences. If you are a teen parent, please know that DAPI is here to support you. You are not only capable but destined for success.

YOUR INFLUENCE
INSPIRES ME TO BREAK THIS CYCLE.

I am immensely proud of our DAPI authors. DAPI Daughters, your stories are a beacon of hope and resilience.

With deep admiration,

Doris L. P. Griffin, Ed.D.

Executive Director

YOUR INFLUENCE
INSPIRES ME TO BREAK THIS CYCLE.

YOUR INFLUENCE
INSPIRES ME TO BREAK THIS CYCLE.

SHIFTING PATHS

Written by: Ta'Shay Todd

YOUR INFLUENCE
INSPIRES ME TO BREAK THIS CYCLE.

SHIFTING PATHS

By: Ta'Shay Todd

Hard, sad, and tough are the words I would use to describe my childhood, growing up without my dad. Too many times, I heard the phrase, "I'm coming to see you, I'll be there to pick you up, or I'm taking you out." Almost every time he uttered those words, I would instantly get excited until I realized those phrases had no truth or meaning. I've lost count of how many times I've waited and waited or called him and got no response. Over time, I developed trust issues, finding it hard to believe in anyone. I began to feel that if I couldn't trust my dad, I couldn't trust anyone. My dad had lied and broken me down so many times that I couldn't stand to experience that treatment from anyone else. I closed myself off from everyone and rarely opened up to trust again.

I tried to block out the heavy beating of my heart and the disappointing thoughts of my

YOUR INFLUENCE
INSPIRES ME TO BREAK THIS CYCLE.

dad, but anytime I saw other people with their dads, my hurt would surface again. I fought through my emotions alone. No one had the right actions or words to help me get through my pain. I would express my emotions with tears or writing how I felt. As I became a teenager, I smoked more than I should have and drank my pain away. After each puff or sip, my problems felt solved; it was like I had nothing to worry about. It felt like all my pain was gone, but that was just another way of blocking everything out like it never happened.

I never allowed people to love me correctly. I didn't need their love, so I thought. I had a selfish way of thinking. It was only about me when a situation would arise until I met my daughter's father. My daughter's father makes me feel loved and happy. Even through our ups and downs, he always makes sure I am alright. To this day, the hurt from my dad is still present, and some days it can be rough; however, I really appreciate my daughter's father.

YOUR INFLUENCE INSPIRES ME TO BREAK THIS CYCLE.

As my daughter's father and I prepare for the arrival of our baby girl, it's important that we break the "Fatherless" child cycle. I don't want our daughter out here in the real world looking for love from a guy that her dad never gave her. I've always wanted to experience a daddy-daughter dance, school field trips with him in attendance, and even watch a movie with my dad, but I couldn't. He acted like I never existed. I never want her to feel the hurt I felt. As it relates to her father, I would only want the feelings of sadness, mistreatment, selfishness, and nonexistent to be figments of her imagination. I know what I want for her through her father is mostly in his power; however, I will try my best to make things manageable. My goal is never to let anything that happens between him and me get to her, to practice trusting him and his actions as her father, and lastly, to stop accusing and arguing with him. I believe the more I allow her father to do his part, she would never feel how I felt about not having my dad.

YOUR INFLUENCE
INSPIRES ME TO BREAK THIS CYCLE.

I know my journey of missed moments with my dad doesn't end because I'm now a mom. So, I will keep working on myself to open up more and become emotionally available for myself and my daughter's well-being. In and out of my personal healing journey, I will always be present for my daughter, cheering her on when the days are tough and letting her know that it's okay. I will always be here for her, no matter what.

Growing up without having my dad wasn't easy or fun; however, that didn't stop life for me. It taught me a valuable lesson about how important it is to be present in my daughter's life. I must keep thriving! We must keep thriving! To every fatherless girl, always remember that you got this. Please don't let the mistakes of someone else make you believe that you're not good enough or question if you're the reason or problem. Through it all, I know we can come out stronger.

YOUR INFLUENCE
INSPIRES ME TO BREAK THIS CYCLE.

YOUR INFLUENCE
INSPIRES ME TO BREAK THIS CYCLE.

MY TRUE

HIS FUTURE

Written by: Jordyn Sephes

YOUR INFLUENCE
INSPIRES ME TO BREAK THIS CYCLE.

MY TRUTH, HIS FUTURE

By: Jordyn Sephes

As a little girl, I always felt that people used yelling as the only method to get their point across. I don't want my child to feel the way I felt or take on the behaviors I displayed when faced with yelling, as it's simply not healthy. I don't want my child to feel like he can't come to me because he believes I will yell.

Yelling doesn't get the point across; instead, it causes fear and intimidation. Personally, when I was repeatedly yelled at, it caused me to go mute, it increased my anxiety, and I isolated myself. Currently, if someone were to yell at me, I'd start crying and get mad; I still battle with this trait.

I plan not to yell at my son for everything. Instead, I'll ask questions to understand his actions and reactions better. I'll focus on recognizing my triggers and thinking before I react while setting clear expectations. I

YOUR INFLUENCE INSPIRES ME TO BREAK THIS CYCLE.

know I will yell at times. I'm human, and sometimes it's hard to control. However, I understand that I don't need to resort to yelling and intimidating my child or anyone else.

I'm committed to breaking the cycle now. My child is innocent and shouldn't feel yelling is the only way to deliver a message. A significant takeaway from my story is that regardless of your upbringing, it's possible to overcome and become a better person for yourself and your children. Ultimately, you don't always need to yell for your message to be understood.

YOUR INFLUENCE
INSPIRES ME TO BREAK THIS CYCLE.

YOUR INFLUENCE
INSPIRES ME TO BREAK THIS CYCLE.

FOR THE SON I CARRIED, FOR THE FATHER I LOST

Written by: Carmela Martin

YOUR INFLUENCE INSPIRES ME TO BREAK THIS CYCLE.

FOR THE SON I CARRIED, FOR THE FATHER I LOST

By: Carmela Martin

At a very young age, my father passed away, leaving me empty inside. I never had a chance to grow up with him. I questioned why he had to leave. That question sat heavy in my heart. At seven years old, I didn't know death meant physically gone. I thought he would come back eventually, but as I got older and realized that my dad still hadn't returned, I began to understand that it meant he was physically gone forever, which caused me to react to his death in the present time as if it just happened. I would cry every day. Tears would pour from my eyes out of nowhere. The more I cried, the less I wanted to be around people. I always wanted to be left alone.

At home, when my mom brought a new boyfriend around, I rejected him. It felt like no one could or should try to take my dad's place. At school, I found it hard to focus.

YOUR INFLUENCE
INSPIRES ME TO BREAK THIS CYCLE.

My mind would drift, and sadness would creep in when I saw my classmates laughing with their dads. I envied those moments, wondering what it would be like to have that bond. In my loneliness, I started looking for pieces of that fatherly love in boys around me, hoping someone could fill the space he left behind.

When the time felt right, I planned for my pregnancy. I had always hoped that my first child would be a boy. When I learned my child's gender, I was overwhelmed with joy! The happiness I felt was pure, knowing I was having a son. I believed that having my son would fill the void of love that my father couldn't express. However, my perspective has changed over time. I now understand that the bond my son and I share is unconditional, and while I can't bring my father back, it's not my son's responsibility to mend my fatherless wounds. As his mother, I want to protect and free him from that burden I once placed on him.

If I had a relationship with my dad, I might not have felt so lost or confused about who I

YOUR INFLUENCE
INSPIRES ME TO BREAK THIS CYCLE.

was. Maybe I wouldn't have looked for that connection with other people, especially with boys who could never really fill that space. I wouldn't have felt so alone watching other kids with their fathers, wondering why I couldn't have that, too. I never want my son to endure such a heartbreaking loss or experience the emotions I felt from not having my dad, whether from death or the absence of his father.

I imagine that if my dad had been here, life would have felt more complete. Maybe I would've grown up with more security, knowing he was there to protect and guide me. I picture him cheering me on at school events, teaching me life lessons, or simply being there on quiet days when I needed someone to talk to. From the many wonderful stories I've heard about my father, I believe I would've felt more grounded. School might've been easier to focus on. My emotions might've been easier to handle. And maybe, just maybe, I would've grown up with less of a hole in my heart. If it was solely up to me, I would make sure my son

YOUR INFLUENCE INSPIRES ME TO BREAK THIS CYCLE.

receives everything mentioned above from his father.

I know that my son will always need his father, not because he'll always know what to do, but because he'll teach him how to fly when the wind comes, and he'll possess the teachings I lack as a woman. I always want to nurture my son's bond with his father. I will create space, show support, and choose love over resentment. I may not control everything, but I will always choose what's best for his heart. Continuing to see what's best for my son through my experiences will benefit us as a family. I pray my son will know the love of his father and never question if he's worthy of it.

While our experiences shape who we become, they don't have to dictate the love and lasting impact we have on future generations. We all have it in us to be the change we want to see. I'm sure my son will appreciate me.

YOUR INFLUENCE
INSPIRES ME TO BREAK THIS CYCLE.

YOUR INFLUENCE
INSPIRES ME TO BREAK THIS CYCLE.

THE BEGINNING OF MY JOURNEY AS A GIRL MOM

Written by: Yamia Brown

*YOUR INFLUENCE
INSPIRES ME TO BREAK THIS CYCLE.*

THE BEGINNING OF MY JOURNEY AS A GIRL MOM

By: Yamia Brown

Girl Mom: A female that gives birth to a daughter.

Girl moms often face criticism, with comments that frame having a daughter as a burden instead of a blessing. I'm simply a girl who has been fortunate enough to embrace the journey of motherhood as a girl mom.

My reaction to learning my child's gender was similar to most of the population: "Raising a girl is a challenge." I instantly assumed it would be hard and reflected on my attitude, which I hope she doesn't adopt. However, I believe that if I nurture a strong relationship with her, her attitude will be more positive. My goal is to create a great bond with my daughter, as I didn't experience that with my mother.

YOUR INFLUENCE
INSPIRES ME TO BREAK THIS CYCLE.

Throughout my childhood, my relationship with my mom was never very strong. She was rarely around, and as I grew older, I didn't talk to her about much. I felt I couldn't speak to her about anything that was going on in my life. She was usually busy with work or caring for my little sister, which made me feel like she wasn't truly there for me. I began to think she didn't like me as much, which fueled my anger. In search of attention, I started to leave the house and act out. I want to break that cycle with my daughter.

As a girl myself, I know that the teenage years can be tough, and I often think about the constant challenges I may face while raising her. But before we get to that vulnerable phase in her life, I will prioritize her emotional security. Our bond has already begun. I read and talk to my sweet girl and speak words of positivity and comfort while she's in my womb. But my commitment doesn't stop there. I'll continue to read and talk to her when she's born. I'll balance out the time we spend together and make life fun with sensory boards and

YOUR INFLUENCE
INSPIRES ME TO BREAK THIS CYCLE.

playtime with her. For every milestone she reaches, I will be there to encourage, cheer, support, and guide her. As she grows and begins to recall memories, she will know I am always there for her.

I want my daughter to feel secure in coming to me about anything and to understand that our bond is unbreakable. Our respect for one another will be mutual, and I will trust her as she trusts me. I won't need to stress or overthink her outings; I will have faith in the child I have raised and the relationship we have built. There will be no need to worry when she does certain things because our relationship will display compassion first, integrity, responsibility, and trust.

There's a difference between having a child and raising a child. My aunt raised me and taught me the positive impact a bond can have on a child. Her support and love for me have never changed, which makes me confident that if I am the lifeline for my daughter that my aunt was for me, we will be just fine.

YOUR INFLUENCE
INSPIRES ME TO BREAK THIS CYCLE.

To everyone reading my story, my key message is this: never allow the opinions of others to affect your mental state. When people offer advice, be cautious not to let them manipulate you into making decisions against your will. For example, many individuals disapprove of my choice not to vaccinate my daughter and are attempting to sway me into changing my mind. Remember, there's no need to feel guilty for choosing what you believe is best rather than conforming to someone else's expectations.

YOUR INFLUENCE
INSPIRES ME TO BREAK THIS CYCLE.

YOUR INFLUENCE
INSPIRES ME TO BREAK THIS CYCLE.

UNPLANNED BLESSINGS

AND

VALUABLE LESSONS

Written by: Ava Kerwin

YOUR INFLUENCE
INSPIRES ME TO BREAK THIS CYCLE.

UNPLANNED BLESSINGS

AND

VALUABLE LESSONS

By: Ava Kerwin

As a young girl, full of life with dreams bigger than my height, I never would have imagined myself being pregnant at sixteen. Almost every adult's favorite question to ask a child is, "What do you want to be when you grow up?" and my answer was always a nurse. My dreams were dreamt beyond the years of my teens and straight into adulthood until the day everything came to a standstill. One day, I'm going out with friends and having fun; the next, I'm learning that I'm pregnant.

It was a morning that I will never forget. I woke up feeling sick. My immediate thought was, I have the Flu, but far in the back of my mind, the idea of being pregnant was loud. My mother asked me to fulfill a DoorDash order for her. While doing so, I snuck in a

YOUR INFLUENCE
INSPIRES ME TO BREAK THIS CYCLE.

pregnancy test. Convincing myself that it would be negative, I took some time before peeing on the stick. Two lines appeared immediately! I was shocked! It took weeks of processing that I really was pregnant. Once reality hit me, many thoughts went through my mind. I thought about my baby's gender, becoming a mom, and, most importantly, the relationship I wanted to build with my child.

As the days turned into weeks and the weeks turned into months, my mind began processing the ways I can show up for my child before she arrives. Sometimes, the hardest thing to do is remove people from my life that aren't good for me, but I know it's important to do it now. I must take care of myself first to be prepared to care for the well-being of my child. The last thing I want to do is be in a state of distress, causing bad emotions to transfer to my baby. A healthy and happy pregnancy is my priority. I understand that any emotion that affects me will affect my baby in a good or bad way, now or in our future.

YOUR INFLUENCE
INSPIRES ME TO BREAK THIS CYCLE.

As I write this story, I'm unaware of my child's gender; however, I hope it's a girl. During my childhood, I craved a perfect fairytale relationship with my mom. My childhood wasn't all bad, but if it were up to me, I would have wanted my mom to voice her love for me more. For us to have mommy and daughter dates, argue less, and have intimate moments of me coming to her in confidence. I'm almost sure that it was never my mom's intention to make me feel the way I did as a child. She was doing what was necessary to rebuild her life. I was just caught in the middle during the process. It's important for me to work on myself now to break the cycle for my child. My goal is to create a relationship with my child that I wanted with my mom at a young age, whether it's a girl or boy, but I hope you're a girl.

Many emotions held me hostage growing up. I was forced to adjust to new environments as I changed schools from going back and forth between my mom's and grandparents' homes. I would take my anger out on my grandparents and the people that

YOUR INFLUENCE
INSPIRES ME TO BREAK THIS CYCLE.

were there for me. I stopped going to school and lost focus. Nothing seemed to help move me ahead. I felt stuck. I never want my child to feel stuck in a hole with no way out. It's my duty to prepare myself mentally for the challenges she may face.

During my moments of emptiness, introducing positive language into my life eventually helped. I will work on my language as a mother by speaking words of beauty and wisdom to my stomach as it grows and to my child during every stage of development. If something is done wrong, I never want to use bashing words. I am confident that if I keep working on myself, I will create a space of safety, understanding, and trust. My child will trust that it is okay to come to me, that her words won't fall on deaf ears, and that there's no reason to be sneaky because she will have mommy's grace to guide them. I will be the best person for my child to come to.

As my child and I grow together, she will watch me closely. One day, our little world will make sense to her. I hope she cherishes

YOUR INFLUENCE
INSPIRES ME TO BREAK THIS CYCLE.

the memories of me having her back and develops an ambitious mindset, knowing I'll always be there to support her with any choice she makes.

To the person that's reading my story, thank you. I once felt stuck but didn't let it stop me. As a new mom, I have a stronger sense of motivation. I will continue to do my best for me and my child. If you ever feel stuck, believe that it does get better with time. Remember, there is always a way out. You must want it.

YOUR INFLUENCE
INSPIRES ME TO BREAK THIS CYCLE.

YOUR INFLUENCE
INSPIRES ME TO BREAK THIS CYCLE.

YOUR INFLUENCE
INSPIRES ME TO BREAK THIS CYCLE.

BREAKING THE CYCLE: A PROMISE TO MY CHILD

Written by: Daniela Morales

YOUR INFLUENCE INSPIRES ME TO BREAK THIS CYCLE.

BREAKING THE CYCLE: A PROMISE TO MY CHILD

By: Daniela Morales

As a child, I was always torn between my parents. I felt useless. My parents would constantly argue back and forth over the phone. While my mom wanted my dad to pick me up, my dad would deny showing up for me because I was allegedly another man's child. I felt left out of the family. I wanted both parents in my life. When I needed my mom the most, she refused to talk to me; she thought I would tell her that I wanted my dad. And when I needed my dad, he never showed up.

I used to believe that my mom only wanted to share her time with my brothers, which upset me. I would hit her in public, talk back to her, and say hurtful things that included me wanting to end my life and go live with my dad. I've tried to end my life because I wanted attention from my mom. My actions often made my mom cry.

YOUR INFLUENCE INSPIRES ME TO BREAK THIS CYCLE.

I tried to find the love my dad never gave me in boys while being selfish towards my mom and brothers. I don't want my kid to do to me the things I did to my mom. I also don't want my child to look for his dad and be waiting for him just for him not to show up.

While pregnant, I practice enjoying the moment and avoiding anything that can add stress to my baby. I want to learn from the sad moments while enjoying every moment of laughter. Learning how to be present for my son in ways I wasn't shown up for will bring me comfort and my son support. He'll know he has me if he ever needs someone to talk to. He'll be able to trust that I won't tell anyone about our conversations. I'll let him know the good that comes when you learn from your mistakes and appreciate the people you have. You never know when you are going to need them.

YOUR INFLUENCE
INSPIRES ME TO BREAK THIS CYCLE.

YOUR INFLUENCE
INSPIRES ME TO BREAK THIS CYCLE.

WHERE DOES BIG EMOTIONS GO

Written by: Deja Perry

YOUR INFLUENCE
INSPIRES ME TO BREAK THIS CYCLE.

WHERE DOES BIG EMOTIONS GO

By: Deja Perry

Where do big emotions go when there's no outlet to express yourself? For me, this caused layers of rage to show up in my actions. As a new mom, I want to break that cycle for my son and teach him that it's okay to have emotions and express them.

The reputation that boys get for showing emotion symbolizes weakness. They're often told that crying is for girls or that they can't be sad because they must protect and provide. "Man up" is the term used when any young boy or man is at his breaking point. I don't want my son to keep in his feelings until he explodes with emotion. I also don't want him to feel ashamed of having emotion or that it's wrong. I don't want his future relationships to suffer because he doesn't know that communication is good.

YOUR INFLUENCE
INSPIRES ME TO BREAK THIS CYCLE.

Growing up, I was sexually abused from age five to eleven and once again at fourteen. I didn't tell anybody; I felt no one would believe me. At one point, I would tell my dad anything and everything, but I couldn't tell him that I was abused. The thought of getting in trouble or that I wouldn't be believed caused me to go mute. I carried around feelings of confusion and fear and never had the opportunity to gather the courage to tell my dad.

My dad passed away from brain cancer when I was eleven, and the relationship I had with my mom wasn't good; I barely knew her. She passed away when I was ten.

My dad was my person, the man I trusted the most, so when he died, I didn't know what I was feeling. I felt guilty for attempting to talk about my emotions. I believed that I shouldn't talk about my feelings if it weren't with him- plus, I always felt like everyone else was going through more, so opening up would just make everything worse.

YOUR INFLUENCE
INSPIRES ME TO BREAK THIS CYCLE.

My family would tell me to get over it, and several therapists later in my grief journey said to me that after so long, grief should be better or that certain reactions I had shouldn't have made me feel the way they did. All that did was make me feel that there was something wrong because I couldn't get over the loss of my father as quickly as everyone else. Anytime I tried to express my feelings, I would lie. I lied so that my reason for being upset was justified and not shamed or deemed as untrustworthy.

After years of keeping my feelings in, I exploded and experienced a mental breakdown for a year and a half, which led to me making multiple attempts on my life, cutting my wrist, and using substances. I had all these feelings and didn't know what to do with them. On top of that, I was in and out of shelters and foster homes by the age of fourteen. Being overwhelmed with my emotions caused me to run away several times. I eventually dropped out of school. I never want my son to experience a mental breakdown from holding back his feelings.

YOUR INFLUENCE
INSPIRES ME TO BREAK THIS CYCLE.

I enrolled myself back in school for my son, and I prioritized breaking the cycle of an emotionless young boy. I will always provide a judge-free zone where we can vent, talk, or cry, but I will also tell him that not everyone deserves to see his vulnerability and teach him how to tell who is a good person to talk to and who isn't. In my actions with others, I can show him that it's okay to express his feelings while also creating a space of comfort. While everything is not in my control, while things are, I will make sure that he's only around supportive people regardless of whether it is family or not. I want to be sure that my son is always supported anywhere he goes.

YOUR INFLUENCE
INSPIRES ME TO BREAK THIS CYCLE.

YOUR INFLUENCE
INSPIRES ME TO BREAK THIS CYCLE.

MY PROMISE TO HER:

EVOLVING TO BE THE BEST MOM I CAN BE

Written by: Tifani Sanchez-Romero

YOUR INFLUENCE INSPIRES ME TO BREAK THIS CYCLE.

MY PROMISE TO HER:

EVOLVING TO BE THE BEST MOM I CAN BE

By: Tifani Sanchez-Romero

It is for my daughter that I will break the cycle. I want my daughter to know she has me to talk to about anything, such as her struggles, her day, and more, without thinking that I will disregard her feelings or not hear her out. I need to be there to guide her; if she were getting bullied, I wouldn't call her weak, tell her to grow up, or tell her that she is not good enough and that she has to change herself. Instead, I want her to know she can talk to me without feeling embarrassed by her situation, knowing I won't call her names and that she has me there to hear her out, help her, and guide her on any path. I will do my best not to make her feel she needs to change to prove her worth. I will instead tell her to stay encouraged and that she's always worthy. It's important that I give my daughter words of

YOUR INFLUENCE
INSPIRES ME TO BREAK THIS CYCLE.

affirmation daily while letting her know she's more than enough. That will show her I'm always here. I will prioritize quality time with her, making plans for us on my free days, frequently checking up with her, and being involved in her activities or interests.

Growing up, I lived in a small apartment, a two-bedroom, to be exact. There were seven of us: me, my twin, my oldest sister, an aunt who was a teen, my grandma, my mom, and my dad. Money was tight, and we were pretty cramped up. My parents were around; however, they worked a lot.

My siblings and I were usually left with my auntie or often left with our grandma. Going outside to play was never a problem. Kids and teens always surrounded us, but never any grown-ups. When lunch or dinner was ready, my grandma or aunt would call for us but rarely checked on us unless we went inside the house for something, which was rare. We were left with the ability to wander anywhere we chose to go, even if places were off-limits. Whenever my mom or dad was home, they were physically present but

YOUR INFLUENCE
INSPIRES ME TO BREAK THIS CYCLE.

unavailable. Their presence was only useful for telling us what to do or not to do or when to return to the house.

My dad was always glued to the computer and doing his DJ stuff. He would blast music to the max volume with his headphones on, to the point we could hear. His work occupied his full attention. My sister and I would check in with him rather than him checking up on us. We often had to yell and scream, tap him on the shoulder more than once, probably for a good minute, or stand next to the screen. He still didn't notice unless we waved our hands across his screen. It was difficult for him to acknowledge our presence whenever he was deep into his DJ stuff. He was around the house but wasn't there for us.

My mom was always out doing work. When she started to do her Zumba classes and made it her job, my sister and I would go with her to help, watch her work, or get involved. She'd tell us what to do but lacked the emotional support we needed. She would tell us what or what not to do but instantly

YOUR INFLUENCE
INSPIRES ME TO BREAK THIS CYCLE.

go back and focus on what she was doing and forget what she had told us. When I went to school and had events, she didn't show. When it came to school check-ups, she sat there and acted like she cared, but she didn't. As soon as we left, she would go on with her day like nothing.

My siblings and I would often come home to nobody. We would stay outside all day until someone returned. In most cases, my older sister, who was two years older, was in charge of the house key. Whenever she forgot her key, we had to find a place to stay. Luckily, we had family around the apartment complex. We would stay in our families' houses. It ended up being an all-day stay until it got dark.

The absence of my parents didn't only affect me; it affected my sisters as well. Whenever we're left alone, my sisters and I will go on many rants about how we were treated differently and how unfair it was. We would compare our perspectives on how we grew up or the need to always speak up just to laugh it off as if it were nothing.

YOUR INFLUENCE INSPIRES ME TO BREAK THIS CYCLE.

Furthermore, I felt I couldn't talk to my parents about anything whenever I encountered a bad situation. I always felt they wouldn't care or even bother to listen to what I was going through. I felt like I had no one, and once I saw other kids with their parents, I would look at them funny or have a heart-dropping feeling.

Whenever my younger siblings are up to something in front of my mom, we usually like to call it out and ask our mom why she doesn't imply things she implemented on us when we were younger. We would discuss how different things are and advise her to apply those old rules. But after we speak our peace, I usually laugh and disregard what was said because I feel like those words don't matter anymore now that I'm "older," but deep down, sometimes I wish we got the treatment they get.

I understand that it may take time to recognize the positive impact of my presence in my daughter's life, especially since I haven't experienced what it feels like to have someone consistently there for me. It

YOUR INFLUENCE
INSPIRES ME TO BREAK THIS CYCLE.

will require patience to see how I contribute to her emotional, mental, and physical well-being in her daily life. However, even if there isn't immediate changes, I won't give up. I realize that much of what I instill in her will take time to process and grow. This journey is not just about being there for my daughter; it's also about my own growth as a mother and as a person, as I work to break a cycle that slightly still affects me. I'll practice being patient and kind to myself during this process. As a mother, I will constantly give myself reassurance and words of affirmation, reminding myself not to let the feelings that I experienced with my parents in the past get in the way of me changing this cycle. I will do my best to continue learning, maturing, and attending to myself to be there for my daughter.

I want others to learn that there's a difference between your presence and being present in your child's life. Just because you stay and sit with them in the same room doesn't mean your child is getting that emotional and mental connection with you. It is important to be part of your child's life.

YOUR INFLUENCE INSPIRES ME TO BREAK THIS CYCLE.

Being present will help them grow and learn faster. They will trust you in any circumstance, have hope, know they have someone who will be there for them emotionally and mentally, and not be scared to open up to you as a parent openly.

YOUR INFLUENCE
INSPIRES ME TO BREAK THIS CYCLE.

YOUR INFLUENCE
INSPIRES ME TO BREAK THIS CYCLE.

YOUR INFLUENCE
INSPIRES ME TO BREAK THIS CYCLE.

BABY STEPS ON BRAND NEW TRAILS

Written by: Hayden McCall-Ross

YOUR INFLUENCE
INSPIRES ME TO BREAK THIS CYCLE.

BABY STEPS ON BRAND NEW TRAILS

By: Hayden McCall-Ross

Growing up, I was surrounded by smokers: my mom, dad, uncle, and older cousins. Because of this, I developed asthma at a young age, impacting my quality of life. My mom often spent a lot of her time outside in her car smoking rather than spending time with me.

By the age of seven, I'd seen plenty of commercials about how smoking was dangerous and could cause lung cancer. I was usually scared, upset, and angry. I didn't want anything to happen to my mother as a result of her smoking. My sisters and I would beg her to stop, but she wouldn't. For my son, I want to break this cycle now, starting with me. I do not smoke or do any substances, and I hope when my child gets older, he will follow the same path.

YOUR INFLUENCE INSPIRES ME TO BREAK THIS CYCLE.

I don't want my son to think smoking is normal or healthy. His well-being comes first; if it's within my control, he won't be around anyone who will expose him to it. I will inform others of my wishes and ask if they'll accommodate our needs. If they simply can't, I'll do everything within my power to avoid those who can't respect our boundaries. I want to raise my son around healthy habits, so he's not influenced by bad ones.

Breaking this cycle will benefit me, my son, and his father. Both I and his father have grown up around substance users. We don't want our child to experience the things we did as children. Our goal is to create a healthy, happy, structured family. We will teach our son about the dangers of smoking when he's old enough to understand. We'll explain the physical risks it can have on your body, the addiction to it, and ways it can strain relationships. I will also explain why I decided to keep him away from it.

YOUR INFLUENCE INSPIRES ME TO BREAK THIS CYCLE.

I want others to see that you can end a cycle at any point when you truly want to. I want this story to show people that they can have the strength for their children and/or themselves to stay away from people who use substances, even if it's been a part of their environment for a long time.

YOUR INFLUENCE
INSPIRES ME TO BREAK THIS CYCLE.

YOUR INFLUENCE
INSPIRES ME TO BREAK THIS CYCLE.

YOUR INFLUENCE
INSPIRES ME TO BREAK THIS CYCLE.

THIS I BELIEVE

Written by: Nathalie Alvarado

YOUR INFLUENCE
INSPIRES ME TO BREAK THIS CYCLE.

THIS I BELIEVE

By: Nathalie Alvarado

From 2023 to 2024, times became rough. I became a mother at fifteen, with no knowledge of how to manage or be stable enough for my daughter. I experienced challenge after challenge. My daughter's father and I were off and on, my relationship with my father wasn't great, and I was losing focus and track of myself. However, since giving birth to my daughter, Lina, my life has become the biggest blessing I could ever ask for. I've changed a lot. My personality has flourished beautifully. I became stronger, learned who I am for myself, got my mindset back on track, and started thinking more maturely.

I was never a school person; I hated school so much. I was over it. I dropped out for almost one year in 10th grade and never planned to return. After learning I was pregnant, I planned to get my GED. But after a year had passed and my kid was

YOUR INFLUENCE
INSPIRES ME TO BREAK THIS CYCLE.

finally born, I decided to go back to school; however, it took me some time because I just wasn't ready. I found a program called Delaware Adolescent Program (DAPI) for teen expectant mothers or teenage mothers who had their babies. Before starting at DAPI, I changed my thoughts about attending school. My life wasn't just about me anymore; my choice to go back was for my baby girl. I was determined to continue my education for her! And I am beyond grateful that I didn't give up on myself. Whenever I feel like giving up, my first thought is ALWAYS, ALWAYS, my child because her priorities come first. I want my child to see me as something in life. I want her to witness what it looks like for her mother not to give up, and when things get hard for her, she doesn't give up but keeps trying even if it gets hard. After continuing with school for two years, I'm proud to say I'm a senior graduating this year of 2025!

Although it wasn't easy, I did it! I started, stopped, and started again to get where I am. Remember that it's okay to start over again when breaking any cycle. As a 17-year-old

YOUR INFLUENCE
INSPIRES ME TO BREAK THIS CYCLE.

mother raising a 1-year-old, I'm very blessed to have my Lina. Lina, without you, I would not know where I would be, literally. I was at my lowest, and you gave me the strength to learn who I am again and that I can be better. You showed me that I could be a person, have patience, and love myself again. I hope you realize that everything I do is for you.

I want to acknowledge my father. Earlier, I mentioned that we didn't have a great relationship, but I am proud to say things have changed. Dad, thank you for everything you have done for me. If you read my story in the previous book, "My Side of the Story," you know that my father and I had a distant relationship. There was no communication or love for each other, and we barely saw each other, but since I had my daughter, she brought us closer together. Yes, he went without talking to me for five months, but I never gave up on us. I felt desperate without my father; it felt like I was never going to see or speak to him again. I tried and tried until we finally talked and apologized to each other. We now

YOUR INFLUENCE
INSPIRES ME TO BREAK THIS CYCLE.

understand each other's feelings and have finally made a connection. We've built the best relationship I could ask for! Now, my father finally speaks to me. We show love towards each other, and lastly, he loves my daughter! My baby has the best grandpa ever, and I wouldn't trade it for anyone.

My relationship with Lina's father was rocky, but we grew stronger over time. My boyfriend was not good at communication, making it hard for us to understand each other. I set boundaries, and now we're living together in a new home. We are happy and healthy, focusing on our daughter and understanding each other better.

Now, Mom, don't think I forgot about you. You are my inspiration forever and ever. I'm thankful for you always and will always appreciate you for being here for me during my tough times. You're the best grandma my daughter could ever ask for. I love you!

2025 is my year! I'm proudly graduating and logging off to continue pursuing my passion in nursing. I hope everyone who reads my story takes this as an inspiration that life can

YOUR INFLUENCE INSPIRES ME TO BREAK THIS CYCLE.

be tough. Everyone goes through the toughest times, but it will get better, trust me! Time and patience are all you need. My advice to all you teen mommies out there: "Before you give up, think about who's behind you watching." Until next time.

2025' Nathalie Alvarado

YOUR INFLUENCE
INSPIRES ME TO BREAK THIS CYCLE.

YOUR INFLUENCE
INSPIRES ME TO BREAK THIS CYCLE.

YOUR INFLUENCE
INSPIRES ME TO BREAK THIS CYCLE.

BREAKING CYCLES

Message from Ms. Roniesha Seaton

YOUR INFLUENCE
INSPIRES ME TO BREAK THIS CYCLE.

BREAKING CYCLES

By: Ms. Roniesha Seaton

Breaking a cycle isn't always easy. It takes patience, commitment, and practice to see results. It comes with lots of added pressure from yourself and those around you. You'll want to give up, justify why it's okay to continue living on a path of distraction, and encounter emotions you have never felt before. All of the statements mentioned above are equivalent to progress.

As it gets hard, remember your why. It's okay to take breaks, but please don't ever give in. Your decision to break any cycle benefits you and anyone who comes behind you. You have the tools to conquer. Make yourself proud.

Love, Ms. Roniesha Seaton.

YOUR INFLUENCE
INSPIRES ME TO BREAK THIS CYCLE.

YOUR INFLUENCE
INSPIRES ME TO BREAK THIS CYCLE.

YOUR INFLUENCE
INSPIRES ME TO BREAK THIS CYCLE.

TREASURED MEMORIES

YOUR INFLUENCE
INSPIRES ME TO BREAK THIS CYCLE.

YOUR INFLUENCE
INSPIRES ME TO BREAK THIS CYCLE.

The incredible staff who collaborated with each mother.

YOUR INFLUENCE
INSPIRES ME TO BREAK THIS CYCLE.

Treasured Memories for a Lifetime

YOUR INFLUENCE
INSPIRES ME TO BREAK THIS CYCLE.

Thank you, Dr. Griffin, for the incredible opportunity to support Dapi's Daughters.

YOUR INFLUENCE
INSPIRES ME TO BREAK THIS CYCLE.

Thank you, ladies, for placing your trust in me! This year is all about breaking cycles and creating new beginnings.

Made in the USA
Columbia, SC
15 May 2025